Bloodlines

Hannah Brockbank

Indigo Dreams Publishing

First Edition: Bloodlines
First published in Great Britain in 2017 by:
Indigo Dreams Publishing Ltd
24 Forest Houses
Halwill
Beaworthy
EX21 5UU
www.indigodreams.co.uk

ISBN 978-1-910834-64-0

British Library Cataloguing in Publication Data. A CIP record for this book can be obtained from the British Library.

Designed and typeset in Palatino Linotype by Indigo Dreams.
Cover design by Ronnie Goodyer at Indigo Dreams
Printed and bound in Great Britain by: 4edge Ltd
www.4edge.co.uk

Papers used by Indigo Dreams are recyclable products made from wood grown in sustainable forests following the guidance of the Forest Stewardship Council.

For my mother

I would like to thank my Creative Writing MA workshop for their support and helpful feedback during the creation of these poems, particularly Harriette Boyce, Anne Canning, Maureen Corfield, and Katherine Stern.

I am especially grateful to Stephanie Norgate whose wise words and enthusiasm have set me on a lifelong journey with poetry, and to the rest of the English and Creative Writing Department at the University of Chichester, including Hugh Dunkerley, Naomi Foyle, Alison MacLeod, Stephen Mollett, Karen Stevens, and Dave Swann for their excellent teaching and encouragement. And finally, but by no means least, thanks to Olivier, Harriet, and Charlotte for their love, patience, and understanding.

The poem 'Wallpaper' first appeared in *The London Magazine*.

Bloodlines is Hannah Brockbank's debut collection.

CONTENTS

Myling

The Myling girl has been left by her father
in dark woods to die. Her pale hair has grown dull
under the mulch, where shrews burrow and gnaw
at her fingertips, until she rises, changed.

Now, she can smell the hot blood of lost men;
stray woodcutters and hunters.
She tracks them down. Picks them off one by one.
Who sees her jump on their backs?

They buck and pitch beneath her,
try to discard her again
on impure ground.
She may be dead,
but she won't forget.

She licks sweat off their necks,
clamps blue thighs around their ribs.
She clings to them,
begs for proper burial,
but the weight of her despair
sinks them into the ground.
Their throats choke with dirt.

I wonder now,
if I am dead to you,
should I let go, before you pull me under?

*Mylings feature in Scandinavian folk-belief. They are the spirits of unbaptised
children abandoned in the wilderness by their relations.*

Mongrel
An imagined departure

If this is devotion, I should know it,
curled inside my cavernous duvet,
unshakable, as the man I know traces
the gullied contour of my spine, a curve
of vertebrae, skewed disc, soft tissue
too crumpled to shed tears on, a crooked
legacy left by my swaybacked father who strayed,
tail between his legs, passed pubs, pits,
working men's clubs to London, leaving
my mother at the sink, her hands
fumbling tap tops to stop the blasting
water upsetting cups, the discarded tea bags
leaking iron red seams along the drainer.
Outside, a mongrel waited for snippets, a morsel
of anything to stifle its whippet-thin whine.

A Father Takes His Daughter To The Circus
An imagined encounter

If you go back, you may remember,
that fissure of orange light in the dark;
that moment where it all begins

in the circus tent, as the thrum
of sticks on stretched cowhide grows
into a thick hum. The torch juggler sits

on a nine foot unicycle, so high
that his fingertips can stroke
the gentle slope of the canvas roof.

Up, from the ring, someone throws
a cloth sack to the juggler. He pulls it
over his head, stretches out his arms,

catches a flickering torch, an axe,
a flaming ball of kevlar rope, a spinning
crescent of silver scythe.

One! Two! Three! Four!
It can't be done! It can't be done!
A fizzle of sound sparks

from the stand as he peddles forward,
backward, makes sharp angled lines in the sand.
You watch transfixed, your eyes bright as lamps.

I haven't the heart to tell you about the sack's
eye-level slit, the beveled edged scythe, the paraffin
he holds in his mouth, so he can blow you

a plume of orange fire in the dark.

Wallpaper

I used to think the moon followed me, stalking
behind a picket line of trees, extending fingers
of glassy light towards the car as we carved
along the road to stop by the gate
of coppiced sticks. My legs, log-heavy and pale
as stripped pine, would thud into the dark.
I'd find my feet, lumber to bed, search
for his face in the wallpaper

wait for him to emerge from the flocked foliage
to pad silently into bed. I'd play dead
under his weight, he panted, fur greased with exertion.
I'd watch raindrops strike the pane,
chasing the flash of car lights ghosting the glass
as the man in the moon beamed down, said nothing.

Snake

Twelve years after my father left
I stood inside a red tent,
     my arm linked through my cousin's
        and tugged her close.
        A man with a tattooed face draped a snake
          as thick as his arm
       over our shoulders. Its weight sunk us
   into the sand.
The snake's tapered tail coiled
around our hips
     and bound our pelvises together.
          Its head,
             the size of a balled fist,
             rose to my face.
        I felt the flick of its tongue
     on my cheek
        and the sting of hot piss
               run the length
               of my leg.

Hollow

That winter,
on the school field,
I hollowed out
the settled snow
behind the firs
and lay down
in the depression.

I spread out my arms
and scooped the snow
on top of me
until a mound,
a foot thick,
concealed me
and shielded
my frozen skin
from the sun.

White Noise

In the morning,
I close my eyes
against the light
and listen
for the chime
of my father's voice.

But it doesn't rise,
instead, lies low
under a thick blanket
of white noise.

Once

he must have made
enough sound,
for me
to notice
his silence.

Rook

I heard my father everywhere that evening
as I fell to sleep; a clamorous caw
that surged through my bedroom,
left my paper mobile to circle wildly
in the breeze, lifted me so high,
that I was with him in a beat. Together
we searched through the dusk,
until a volerie amassed overhead,
swung round, dipped behind a tangle of trees.
These birds breed in open country, he said,
eyes fixed into the distance.
They return for their young, even the fallen branchlings
for weeks after they're lost.
           One bird beats the earth at my feet.
This one's lucky, he cooed, swooping it from the ground.
Back in the war days, when people were starvin',
 they used to send the lankest lads to scamper up
 them trees. Tied string round branchling's legs,
 took the length of string back down with them,
 the baby bird still attached; left them to fatten
 before they yanked them from their nest to the pot.
The branchling cradled in his arms thrashed,
its pink gape snapped closed. For a moment, it was mute.
Then my father took off up an elm tree to replace it.
That's no life, he called back.
He shook the branches as he rose,
until I could only see where he'd been,
but not where he was.

Clinton Cards

I don't know why I'm here. The air
is sweet and tight like the ligature
of strawberry liquorice lace tied
around her soft wrist.
Quick! Daddy's coming!
Her cool arm brushes past me.
She lifts a pastel card
from the rack to her chest,
presses its paper-thin sentiment
to her heart, floats down
the aisle and disappears.
I don't know why I'm here.

Relief Cut

I find my blades, a block of flesh
coloured lino; set myself up
to explore images of you.
        Cut away space.
I focus on the remains,
transfer pressure to blade.
Try to gauge your depth
from memory,
but find none,
instead slip, slice
what should stay,
flay my thumb,
let out a howl
for all is lost.

Blue

I try to reproduce the sky, find
its true-blue; flatten out silver tubes
with the heel of my hand, pit phthalo,
against cerulean, until the jar
contains a muted sky, shedding no light
through its curved sides.

Photograph

I'm pacing the concrete length of sea defence.
It's strange to think you were once here.
The photo I've brought for reference,
echoes the rows of villas behind, their cliff-white
stuccoed walls, bow fronted balconies.
In the foreground, your face bends out of shape
as the photo curls in on itself in the breeze.
I hold your captured face in both hands, imagine
how my mother once looked at you,
tucked hair behind your ears with fingers deft
as bird bone on the verge of flight,
but stayed, loving you enough to take your photo,
keep it despite the leak of light strobed across
the film, that stripped your complexion,
stole definition from me.

Nests

I'm hacking into a thicket.

I want to make room,
let light in.
I want to
turn over the loam.

I try not to think
about the wrens
who nest here,
their short lines of flight,
their sweet, rapid chirrup.

Restless cocks built
nest upon nest
in this tangle.
I find fragments
of spotted eggshell,
a russet feather
woven into moss.

I hold a half globe of nest,
wonder how many
you have built
since you left me,
with thoughts as dark
and uncomfortable
as a bed of twigs.

Retreat

I'm here to write about you
in a room with a high ceiling,
to release thoughts upwards,

see how they fly, the mark
they make if they land
on the paper. I want to see

you in that bright white page,
but you dissolve into greyness,
fill the space, press against me,

so when I recall you,
the sound is strange;

d, da, dada, daddy.

You have a name, but it isn't this.

Bloodlines

The midwife scans the waiting room,
calls out my married name.
For a beat or two, I don't grasp it;
a name with tangible history,
felt in the knock of my unborn,
a name with heritage, mapped through counties
with traceable routes.

Blue veined motorways travel my arm,
amass under the soft hollow of my elbow crook.
Slap, slap-slap, she hits vessels to wake
some unconscious part.

She talks genetics.
What about your father's side? A history of stroke?
Cancer? Problems of the heart?
She slides the point under my skin,
lets my blood spill what it knows,
through a thin steel needle.

Blood

The sweet heat of her
seeps through the swaddle
into my chest.

> Her face is masked
> with my blood.

I try to sponge the blood away
but send runnels of water
over her head
and flood the bed.

> My blood is thicker
> than water.
> It doesn't run off.

Human Skeleton

It's not unexpected, in this place of bones,
to find a human skeleton fastened in place,
posed between a Slender Loris,
and a Flying Lemur that's pinned
into an arc of flight.

I step towards your skeleton,
we meet eyeball to socket,
blood and flesh long run off
reveals a jagged fault line,
the meeting of cranial plates,
frontal bone giving way
to hollows as deep as my thumb.

If I could rewind time,
I'd hear you grind ridges into your teeth,
I'd see your eyelids twitch and open
to glare back at me.

But here and now,
I stare at the insides of your drilled bones,
threaded on wire, an intricate beadwork
reassembling everything;
your femur, patella - a smooth pebble
of protection.

Your feet, rooted by steel cables,
imprint soft clay beneath you.
Underneath, the label reads;

Human Being, Humanite, Humanis.
Range: Worldwide
Status: Widespread, and dangerous.

Sand

I leave my children on the beach
with their father.
They're happy shaping sand
over his calves,
carving the excess away
with cupped hands.
I remember
how Hepworth's father
inspired her,
how she strung sculptures
to explore the relation
between parts.
She hated
to carve anything pink
as it brought to mind
flesh and how
her toothed chisel
bruised the hardest stone
leaving white spots
that only the rasp of sand
smoothed away.
I reach up to my face,
trace the contours
of my nose, cheekbones,
earlobes that attach
and wonder,
where does my father end
and where do I begin?

Sucker-Punch

Before you throw in the towel,
you spend most weekends in the ring,
your ear-splitting fists muffled in mittens
laced over your wrists.
Your arms blur in a flurry of punches
cleaving lips and chins apart,
spattering canvas floors with gobs of blood.

You bob, weave, tire too fast,
never notice your opponent's hips turn,
the rising arc of his heavy brown arm.
A sucker-punch cracks your nose.

You squint, blinded by tears,
in front of the changing room mirror.
You plug the bloody fall-out
with twists of paper.

You put on a brave face,
before returning home,
the place, that really beats you.

Pub
An imagined encounter

I wrench the door open,
and stride over the threshold
into the still air.
Dogs lean against tables,
waiting for titbits,
a cool drink - a command
to go home.

My father looks up
and knocks over the salt.
Grains cascade over the table.
He ploughs a line
with his finger,
tells me
drawing a line is easy.
It's knowing
          what side
to be on
          that's hard.

Where do I stand?
I look down,
          turn,
walk out fleet-footed
into the swift air.

Fox

It occurred to me
that you can't leave
without trace.

You've left a mark
        where your claws
have cut
        the mire,
where you tore
into a hare
        and tugged
its hot pluck out
onto the path.

After,
you rubbed
        smooth hollows
into the damp grass
with your long
auburn back
        and raked
at the remains
before vanishing
        under a broken bush.

I know
your stink
carried in
from the North.
        But if the wind turned,
would you know me,
the danger
hunting you from behind?

Grave

I forget how quickly time passes,
these days. I hurry, decide
to take a short cut through
the estate. Not much has changed;
rainwater still pools in the same place
on the tarmac. I step back
onto the pavement, where as a youth,
I cussed, pushed crisp packets
into the privet; behind it, the flats;
their thick, black pipes shin up
the walls, cling like espalier spurs,
to mark off all the floors
to the top, where once, a man
was clubbed to death
by his woman, who couldn't
take it anymore. I stop
by the hedge, see something
between the leaves and litter; a grave
the size of a shoe box
amongst the roots. A miniature
rose struggles for light between
the pickets of an ornamental
fence and a cross of ice cream sticks.
I realise, now, that I'm probably too late.

Porthcurno

I don't think
about the echoes inside
the defence tunnels,
the creak of giant cables
under the sea
transmitting words
along copper
twisted
until there is nothing
left to say.

Only the sound
of waves
invading the shore
make it through
the window,
pounding long
into the night,

until the phone rings,
and I dive into the dark
to get it.
A man's voice
thin and distant says;

Is that you?
Can you hear me?

Porthcurno in Cornwall, has a rich communications history and is also the site of the Telegraph Museum.

Martha

The curator shows me a light boned bird.
It is the length of his leathery hand.
The pale rufous throat no longer bobs.
The small, stuffed head, more buffish blue than grey.
Glass eyes, the colour of dried blood,
puncture its head.
Pillowy feathers yield to my touch.

They used to gather in billions.
Once, a flock 300 miles wide,
blackened the skies above Ontario,
and took hours to pass.
They fed on crops, could drink mid-flight
and roost in trees until the boughs snapped
under their weight.

Hunters sold the pigeons' deep pink breasts
as cut-rate food for slaves.
Their feathers were plucked for dowry beds.
They ruptured the pigeons' carmine eyes
with sharpened sticks;
they were left to stumble, blindly
along the edges of forest,
while airborne pigeons swooped low
expecting food, but found nets
and the slash of blades.
The hunters poked nestlings out of branches.
They shot higher nests down
with blunt arrows.
The young fell,
spilt open on the forest floor,
their mouths leaked crop milk into the dirt.

Martha, the last passenger pigeon, lived on in captivity.
As I leave the museum,
I don't think of her loneliness,
but of her keeper.
How did it feel,
in those final, fleeting moments
to see the last of a survivor, before they disappear?

Quarry

He hurtled earth-bound;
a soaked leather ball
pierced mid-air, thudding

                        down
he lies deflated,
neck loosened,

fog-eyed and squinting
in disbelief.

His breast bone
                   is blown apart,
a creaking truss of splintered ribs
and bruised heart.

There's more
               like him
in the wild-lands,

with airless wings that beat hollow,
grounded and retrieved
between snapping teeth.

He disperses heat as he waits
to be hanged by the neck
until he drops

onto broken patterned tiles.

Falconer

After a long search, I caught sight of you
circling above me, before you perched
on top of a light pole, out of arm's reach.

You'd survived all this time in the wild;
riddled with parasites, survived mid-air collisions
that sent you tumbling, but when I called, you

felt no danger, swooped down on my arm,
my fist-full of diced quail and pulled
at the sinews, released flesh from its bonds.

I walked to the mews house, its smooth white walls,
to stop you damaging your feathers,
laid a silver dish of newborn mice at your feet.

You let me hood you, shield your quick eyes
with leather blinkers to free you from distraction,
so you'd only see me; only see straight.

Wings

I shield my eyes
as you tilt in the sky.
The slant of your wings
carves the light.

For a moment,
your shadow
touches me;

I extend my hand,
hope that you
trust me
not to tie you
down.

Indigo Dreams Publishing
24 Forest Houses
Halwill
Beaworthy
Devon
EX21 5UU
www.indigodreams.co.uk